# CAMBRIDGE LIBRARY COLLECTION

*Books of enduring scholarly value*

## Music

The systematic academic study of music gave rise to works of description, analysis and criticism, by composers and performers, philosophers and anthropologists, historians and teachers, and by a new kind of scholar - the musicologist. This series makes available a range of significant works encompassing all aspects of the developing discipline.

## Some Ancient Christmas Carols, with the Tunes to which They Were Formerly Sung in the West of England

A significant figure in the scientific community of his day, and a mentor to the chemist Sir Humphry Davy and his successor as president of the Royal Society, Davies Gilbert (1767–1839) also represented his native Cornwall in Parliament for almost thirty years. His love of his county and his concern to preserve its customs led him to publish in 1822 this collection of eight Christmas folk carols, the first of its kind, drawing on Cornwall's rich oral tradition. In his preface, Davies paints a heartwarming picture of the Christmas Eves of his childhood when, 'in the evening, cakes were drawn hot from the oven; cyder or beer exhilarated the spirits in every house; and the singing of Carols was continued late into the night'. From 'The Lord at first did Adam make' to 'Let all that are to mirth inclined', these simple ballads reflect the West of England's festive heritage.

Cambridge University Press has long been a pioneer in the reissuing of out-of-print titles from its own backlist, producing digital reprints of books that are still sought after by scholars and students but could not be reprinted economically using traditional technology. The Cambridge Library Collection extends this activity to a wider range of books which are still of importance to researchers and professionals, either for the source material they contain, or as landmarks in the history of their academic discipline.

Drawing from the world-renowned collections in the Cambridge University Library and other partner libraries, and guided by the advice of experts in each subject area, Cambridge University Press is using state-of-the-art scanning machines in its own Printing House to capture the content of each book selected for inclusion. The files are processed to give a consistently clear, crisp image, and the books finished to the high quality standard for which the Press is recognised around the world. The latest print-on-demand technology ensures that the books will remain available indefinitely, and that orders for single or multiple copies can quickly be supplied.

The Cambridge Library Collection brings back to life books of enduring scholarly value (including out-of-copyright works originally issued by other publishers) across a wide range of disciplines in the humanities and social sciences and in science and technology.

# Some Ancient Christmas Carols

with the Tunes to which
They Were Formerly Sung
in the West of England

Davies Gilbert

CAMBRIDGE
UNIVERSITY PRESS

# CAMBRIDGE
## UNIVERSITY PRESS

University Printing House, Cambridge, CB2 8BS, United Kingdom

Published in the United States of America by Cambridge University Press, New York

Cambridge University Press is part of the University of Cambridge.

It furthers the University's mission by disseminating knowledge in the pursuit of
education, learning and research at the highest international levels of excellence.

www.cambridge.org
Information on this title: www.cambridge.org/9781108075299

© in this compilation Cambridge University Press 2014

This edition first published 1822
This digitally printed version 2014

ISBN 978-1-108-07529-9 Paperback

SOME

# ANCIENT

# CHRISTMAS CAROLS,

WITH THE

TUNES TO WHICH THEY WERE FORMERLY SUNG

IN THE

## 𝔚est of 𝔈ngland.

COLLECTED BY

## DAVIES GILBERT, F. R. S. F. A. S. &c.

———

London:

PRINTED BY JOHN NICHOLS AND SON,

25, PARLIAMENT STREET.

———

1822.

# CONTENTS.

# PREFACE.

———◆———

THE following Carols or Christmas Songs were chanted to the Tunes accompanying them, in Churches on Christmas Day, and in private houses on Christmas Eve, throughout the West of England, up to the latter part of the late century.

The Editor is desirous of preserving them in their actual forms, however distorted by false grammar or by obscurities, as specimens of times now passed away, and of religious feelings superseded by others of a different cast. He is anxious also to preserve them on account of the delight they afforded him in his childhood; when the festivities of Christmas Eve were anticipated by many days of preparation, and prolonged through several weeks by repetitions and remembrances.

Christmas Day, like every other great festival, has prefixed to it in the calendar a Vigil or Fast; and in Catholic countries Mass is still celebrated at midnight after Christmas Eve, when austerities cease, and rejoicings of all kinds succeed. Shadows of these customs were, till very lately, preserved in the Protestant West of England. The day of Christmas

Eve was passed in an ordinary manner; but at seven or eight o'clock in the evening, cakes were drawn hot from the oven; cyder or beer exhilarated the spirits in every house; and the singing of Carols was continued late into the night. On Christmas Day these Carols took the place of Psalms in all the Churches, especially at afternoon service, the whole congregation joining: and at the end it was usual for the Parish Clerk to declare, in a loud voice, his wishes for a merry Christmas and a happy new year to all the Parishioners.

None of the sports or gambols, so frequently practised on subsequent days, ever mixed themselves with the religious observances of Christmas Eve. Two of the sports most used in Cornwall were, the one, a metrical play, exhibiting the successful prowess of St. George exerted against a Mahometan adversary; the other a less dignified representation of some transactions at a market or fair.

In the first, Saint George enters accoutred with complete armour, and exclaims,

> " Here come I Saint George,
>      That valiant champion bold,
> And with my sword and spear,
>      I've won three crowns of gold.
> I slew the Dragon, *he*
>      And brought him to the slaughter,
> By which I gained fair Sabra,
>      The King of Egypt's daughter."

The Pagan enters.

    " Here come I the Turkish Knight,
    Come from the Turkish land to fight,
    \*   \*   \*   \*   \*   \*   \*   \*   \*
       \*   \*   \*   \*   \*   \*   \*   bold,
    And if your blood is hot,
    I soon will make it cold."

They fight, the Turkish Knight falls, and rising on one knee,

    " Oh! pardon me, Saint George,
    Oh! pardon me, I crave,
    Oh! give me but my life,
    And I will be thy slave."

Saint George, however, again strikes him down; but immediately relenting, calls out

    " Is there no Doctor to be found,
    To cure a deep and deadly wound?"

A Doctor enters, declaring that he has a small phial filled with the juice of some particular plant, capable of recalling any one to life; he tries, however, and fails : when Saint George kills him, enraged by his want of success. Soon after this the Turkish Knight appears perfectly well; and having been fully convinced of his errors by the strength of Saint George's arm, he becomes a Christian, and the scene closes.

The Fair or Market usually followed, as a Farce. Several persons arranged on benches were sometimes supposed to sell corn; and one applying to each seller in his turn inquired the price, using a set form of words, to be answered in a corresponding manner. If any error were committed, a grave personage was introduced with much ceremony, grotesquely attired, and provided with a large stick; who, after stipulating for some ludicrous reward, such as a gallon of moon-light, proceeded to shoe the untamed colt, by striking the person in error on the sole of the foot.

For an ample account of various customs and ceremonies practised at Christmas in former periods, the Reader is referred to Brand's "Observations on Popular Antiquities," edited by Henry Ellis, F.R.S. and Secretary of the Society of Antiquaries, two vols. 4to.; and to "The Clavis Calendaria, by John Brady," two vols. 8vo. In each of these works will be found a very curious dissertation on the word *yule;* the name of a Pagan festival, which has passed into most European languages, to denominate Christmas. The French *noel* is obviously derived from this word, and appears corrupted into "Now Well," when it forms a part of the Chorus in the fourth Carol; and perhaps indicates the whole to be a translation.

*Tredrea,* 1822.

# POSTSCRIPT.

———◆———

Since the preceding page was printed, a Friend has pointed out to me what is said under the word *Nouel* or *Noel*, in ' Dictionnaire Etymologique de la Langue Françoise, par M. Menage."

" Le Mot de Nouel étoit autrefois un mot de re-jouissance ; on le crioit dans toutes les fêtes et solennités publiques.

" Martial de Paris, à l'entrée du Roy Charles VII. dans Verneuil :

" Ce jour vint le Roy à Verneuil,
Où il fut receu à grand joye
Du peuple joyeux à merveil,
En criant Noel par la voye."

# CAROL 1.

The Lord at first did Adam make Out of the dust & clay

And in his nostrils breathed life E en as the Scriptures say

And then in E dens paradise He placed him to dwell

That he within it should remain To dress & keep it well

✳ These two lines are repeated to the remaining Verse or Burden.
"Then let fond Christians &c.

A

# COLLECTION

OF

# CHRISTMAS CAROLS.

——◆——

## CAROL I.

FOR CHRISTMAS EVE.

### I.

The Lord at first did Adam make
Out of the dust and clay,
And in his nostrils breathed life,
E'en as the Scriptures say.
And then in Eden's Paradise
He placed him to dwell,
That he within it should remain
To dress and keep it well.

Now let good Christians all begin
An holy life to live,
And to rejoice and merry be,
For this is Christmas Eve.

## II.

And then within the garden he
    Commanded was to stay,
And unto him in commandment
    These words the Lord did say :
The fruit which in the garden grows
    To thee shall be for meat,
Except the tree in the midst thereof,
    Of which thou shalt not eat.

## III.

For in the day that thou shalt eat,
    Or do it them come nigh ;
For if that thou doth eat thereof
    Then surely thou shalt die.
But Adam he did take no heed
    Unto that only thing,
But did transgress God's holy law,
    And so was wrapt in sin.

## IV.

Now mark the goodness of the Lord
    Which he for mankind bore,
His mercy soon he did extend,
    Lost man for to restore;
And then for to redeem our souls
    From death and hellish thrall,
He said his own dear son should be
    The Saviour of us all.

## V.

Which promise now is brought to pass,
    Christians, believe it well;
And by the coming of God's dear Son
    We are redeemed from thrall.
Then if we truly do believe,
    And do the thing aright;
Then by his merits we at last
    Shall live in Heaven bright.

## VI.

Now for the blessings we enjoy,
    Which are from Heaven above,
Let us renounce all wickedness
    And live in perfect love.
Then shall we do Christ's own command,
    Ev'n his own written word,
And when we die in Heaven shall
    Enjoy our living Lord.

## VII.

And now the tide is nigh at hand,
    Int' which our Saviour came;
Let us rejoice, and merry be,
    In keeping of the same.
Let's feed the poor and hungry souls,
    And such as do it crave;
Then when we die, in Heaven sure,
    Our reward we shall have.

Now let good Christians all begin
An holy life to live,
And to rejoice and merry be,
For this is Christmas Eve.

# CAROL 2

When God at first cre-a-ted man His Image for to

be And how he made him by his pow'r In

scripture we may see, And how he fram'd his

helpmate Eve The scripture doth us tell Being

## Continued.

free from Sin God plac'd them both in Paradise to

**Chorus.**

dwell    **Let Men** therefore then praise the Lord re-

- joice and cease to mourn Be-- cause our Saviour

Jesus Christ this blessed day was born

## CAROL II.

### I.

WHEN God at first created man
  His image for to be,
And how he made him by his pow'r,
  In Scripture we may see;
And how he framed his helpmate Eve,
  The Scripture doth us tell;
Being free from sin, God placed them both,
  In Paradise to dwell.

#### CHORUS.

Let men, therefore, then praise the Lord,
  Rejoice and cease to mourn,
Because our Saviour Jesus Christ,
  This blessed day was born.

### II.

Man being entered in that place,
  We plainly understand,
The glory of it having seen,
  God gave them this command:
Be sure thou eat not of the tree
  Which in the midst doth stand;
In eating it thou sure shalt die,
  And perish from the land.
          Let men, therefore, &c.

### III.

Man being bless'd in this estate,
    And blessed sure was he,
Having all things at his command,
    But the forbidden tree ;
But then the serpent soon appeared
    To have beguiled Eve,
And said if she should eat thereof
    That she should surely live.
                Let men, therefore, &c.

### IV.

The serpent then hath Eve beguil'd,
    That she thereof did eat;
And likewise gave unto the man,
    As Scripture doth repeat.
And so they both broke God's command,
    Committing of this thing,
Likewise the heavy wrath of God
    Upon them both did bring.——Let men, &c.

### V.

Man being now with grief oppress'd,
    Not knowing where to go ;
His soul before being filled with joy,
    Is now oppress'd with woe.
But see the mercy of the Lord,
    To save man's soul from hell ;
His Son he promised to send down,
    That he with us might dwell.—Let men, &c.

## VI.

An Angel then from Heav'n was sent,
  For to declare God's will,
And to the Virgin Mary came,
  God's words for to fulfil.
A virgin pure of virtuous life,
  Of whom the Lord made choice,
To bear our Saviour in her womb,
  Man's heart for to rejoice.
              Let men, therefore, &c.

## VII.

The Angel then before her stood,
  Declaring of those things,
And told her that she should conceive,
  And bear the King of kings;
To save man's soul from hell beneath,
  From which he could not fly;
For breaking of the Lord's commands
  He was condemned to die.——Let men, &c.

## VIII.

Mary replied, 'tis wondrous strange
  To hear what thou hast said,
I should conceive, being free from sin,
  And still a spotless maid.
The Angel said, 'tis not by man,
  That this should come to pass,
For God himself ordain'd it so
  Before the world ere was.——Let men, &c.

## IX.

This glorious Angel she believ'd,
    That did those tidings bring ;
And then sung praises in her heart
    To God our heav'nly King.
Then God who knew her faith was such
    For to believe aright,
The Angel then by God's own power
    Departed from her sight.
                  Let men, therefore, &c.

## X.

Then Cæsar made a firm decree,
    That certainly should stand,
That all the world should taxed be,
    By the power of this command ;
Mary then being great with child,
    When Cæsar made this call ;
For in her womb conceived was
    The Saviour of us all.——Let men, &c.

## XI.

Then Mary and her husband kind,
    Together did remain,
And went to Bethlehem to be tax'd,
    As Scriptures doth make plain ;
And so it was that they being there,
    Her time being fully come,
Within a stable she brought forth
    Her first-begotten Son.——Let men, &c.

## XII.

God grant us hearts for to believe,
  And likewise to consider,
How that our Saviour suffer'd death,
  Man's soul for to deliver ;
The which, if rightly we believe,
  We shall with him be bless'd,
And when this mortal life is done,
  In Heav'n we hope to rest.

### CHORUS.

Let men, therefore, then praise the Lord,
  Rejoice and cease to mourn ;
Because our Saviour Jesus Christ,
  This blessed day was born.

## CAROL III.

### I.

A virgin most pure, as the prophets do tell,
Hath brought forth a baby as it hath befell,
To be our Redeemer from death, hell, and sin,
Which Adam's transgression had wrapped us in.

#### CHORUS.

Aye, and therefore be you merry,
Rejoice and be you merry;
Set sorrows aside,
Christ Jesus our Saviour was born on this tide.

### II.

In Bethlehem in Jewry a City there was,
Where Joseph and Mary together did pass,
And there to be taxed with many one more,
For Cæsar commanded the same should be so.

Aye, and therefore, &c.

# CAROL 3.

A Virgin most pure as the Prophets do tell, Hath brought forth a baby as it hath befell, To be our redeemer from Death, Hell, and Sin, Which

## Continued.

A‑dams trans‑gressions had wrap‑ped us in Aye and therefore be you mer‑ry Re‑joice and be you merry Set sor‑rows a‑side Christ Je‑sus our Sa‑viour was born on this tide.

## III.

But when they had entered the City so fair,
A number of people so mighty was there;
That Joseph and Mary whose substance was small,
Could find in the Inn there no lodging at all.

> Aye, and therefore, &c.

## IV.

Then were they constrain'd in a stable to lye,
Where horses and asses they us'd for to tie;
Their lodging so simple they took it no scorn,
But against the next morning our Saviour was born.

> Aye, and therefore, &c.

## V.

The King of all kings to this world being brought,
Small store of fine linen to wrap him was sought;
And when she had swadled her young son so sweet,
Within an ox manger she laid him to sleep.

> Aye, and therefore, &c.

## VI.

Then God sent an Angel from Heaven so high,
To certain poor Shepherds in fields where they lye,
And bade them no longer in sorrow to stay,
Because that our Saviour was born on this day.

> Aye, and therefore, &c.

## VII.

Then presently after the Shepherds did spy,
A number of Angels that stood in the sky,
They joyfully talked and sweetly did sing,
To God be all glory our Heavenly King.

### CHORUS.

Aye, and therefore be you merry,
Rejoice and be you merry;
Set sorrows aside,
Christ Jesus our Saviour was born on this tide.

# CAROL 4.

When righteous Joseph wedded was To Israel's Hebrew maid  The Angel Gabriel came from Heav'n And to the vir_gin said  Hail blessed Mary full of grace  The Lord remain on thee

## Continued.

Thou shalt con _ ceive and bear a Son our Saviour for to be Then sing you all both great & small now well now well now well we may re_joice to hear the voice of the An _ gel Gabri _ el.

## CAROL IV.

### I.

When righteous Joseph wedded was
  To Israel's Hebrew maid,
The Angel Gabriel came from Heav'n,
  And to the Virgin said:
Hail, blessed Mary, full of grace,
  The Lord remain on thee;
Thou shalt conceive and bear a Son,
  Our Saviour for to be.

#### CHORUS.

Then sing you all, both great and small,
  Now well, now well, now well;
We may rejoice to hear the voice
  Of the Angel Gabriel.

### II.

'Tis wondrous strange, said Mary then,
  I should conceive and breed,
Being never touched by mortal man,
  But pure in word and deed.
The Angel Gabriel thus reply'd,
  'Tis not the work of man,
But as the Lord in Heav'n decreed,
  Before the world began.—Then sing, &c.

### III.

This Heavenly message she believ d,
    And did to Jury go;
There three months with her friends to stay,
    God's blessed will to show;
And then return'd to Joseph back,
    Her husband meek and mild,
Who thought it strange his wife should be
    Untouch'd and yet with child.

                      Then sing, &c.

### IV.

Then Joseph he to shun the shame,
    Thought her for to forsake,
But then God's Angel in a dream
    His mind did undertake.
Fear not, just Joseph, this thy wife
    Is still a spotless maid;
And not consent of sin, said he,
    Against her can be laid.——Then sing, &c.

### V.

For she is pure, both maid and wife,
    And mother of God's own heir;
The babe of Heav'n and blessed lamb
    Of Israel's flock so fair.
To save lost man from Satan's fold,
    Which Adam lost by thrall,
When first in Eden Paradise
    Did forfeit by the fall.——Then sing, &c.

## VI.

Thus Mary and her husband kind
  Together did remain,
Until the time of Jesus birth,
  As Scriptures doth make plain.
As mother, wife, and virtuous maid,
  Our Saviour sweet conceiv'd;
And in due time to bring us him,
  Of whom we were bereav'd.

Then sing, &c.

## VII.

Sing praises all, both young and old,
  To him that wrought such things;
And all without the means of man,
  Sent us the King of Kings;
Who is of such a spirit bless'd,
  That with his might did quell,
The world, the flesh, and by his death,
  Did conquer death and hell.

### CHORUS.

Then sing you all, both great and small,
  Now well, now well, now well;
We may rejoice to hear the voice
  Of the Angel Gabriel.

# CAROL V.

### I.

Hark! hark! what news the Angels bring,
Glad tidings of a new-born king;
Who is the Saviour of mankind,
In whom we may salvation find.

### II.

This is the day, the blessed morn,
The Saviour of mankind was born;
Born of a maid, a virgin pure,
Born without sin, from guilt secure.

### III.

If Angels sung at Christ's birth,
Sure we have greater cause for mirth;
For why? It was for our sake,
Christ did our human nature take.

### IV.

My soul, learn by thy Saviour's birth,
For to debase thyself on earth;
That thou may'st be exalted high,
To live with him eternally.

# CAROL 5.

Apparantly less Ancient than the others .

## V.

I am resolv'd whilst here I live,
As I'm in duty bound, to give
All glory to the deity,
One God alone, in persons three.

## CAROL VI.

### I.

Whilst Shepherds watched their flocks by night,
  All seated on the ground ;
The Angel of the Lord came down,
  And glory shone all round.

### II.

Fear not, said he, for mighty dread
  Had seized their troubled mind ;
Glad tidings of great joy I bring
  To you and all mankind.

### III.

To you in David's town this day
  Is born of David's line,
A Saviour, which is Christ the Lord,
  And this shall be the sign.

### IV.

The Heav'nly babe you there shall find
  To human view display'd ;
All meanly wrapp'd in swaddling bands,
  And in a manger laid.

# CAROL 6.

Whilst shepherds watch'd their flocks by night

All seat___ed on the ground

The An__gel of the Lord came down

And glo____ry shone all round.

A Psalm Tune.

## V.

Thus spake the seraph, and forthwith
　　Appeared a shining throng
Of Angels, praising God, and thus
　　Addressed their joyful song :

## VI.

All glory be to God on high,
　　And to the earth be peace ;
Good-will henceforth from Heaven to men,
　　Begin and never cease.

# CAROL VII.

## I.

God's dear Son without beginning,
  Whom the wicked Jews did scorn ;
The only wise without all sinning,
  On this blessed day was born :
To save us all from sin and thrall,
  Whilst we in Satan's chains were bound,
And shed his blood to do us good,
  With many a bleeding purple wound.

## II.

Remember then this blessed morning,
  Sweet salvation came unto us ;
When that Christ with grace adorned,
  Gently strove with love to win us,
That mankind should be of God's fold,
  And feed like lambs on Sion's hill ;
Be not unkind, but bear in mind
  How Christ did us remember still.

# CAROL 7

God's &c:   Whom &c:

Th'only &c:   On &c:   To

Whilst &c:   And

With &c:

### III.

In Bethlehem, King David's City,
  Mary's babe had sweet creation;
God and man endu'd with pity,
  And a Saviour of each nation.
Yet Jewry land with cruel hand,
  Both first and last his power denied;
Where he was born they did him scorn,
  And shew'd him malice when he died.

### IV.

No place at all for our Saviour
  In Judea could be found,
Yet sweet Mary's mild behaviour,
  Patiently upon the ground
Her babe did place in vile disgrace,
  Where oxen in their stall did feed;
No midwife mild had this sweet child,
  Nor woman's help at mother's need.

### V.

No kingly robes nor golden treasure,
  Deck'd the birth-day of God's Son;
No pompous train at all took pleasure,
  To this King of kings to run;
No mantle brave could Jesus have,
  Upon his cradle for to lye;
No music charms in nurses arms,
  To sing the babe a lullaby.

## VI.

Yet as Mary sat in solace
  By our Saviour's first beginning,
Hosts of Angels from God's palace,
  Sounding sweet from Heaven singing.
Yea Heaven and earth at Jesus birth,
  With sweet melodious tunes abound ;
And every thing in Jewry's King
  Upon the earth gave cheerful sound.

## VII.

Heav'ns perceiving small befriending
  Of this promis'd prince of might,
From the christal skies descending,
  Blazing glorious beams of light.
A glorious star did shine so far,
  That all the earth might see the same ;
And nations strange their faith did change,
  To yield him honour, laud, and fame.

## VIII.

Then with Angel love inspired,
  The wise princes from the East,
To Bethlehem as they desired,
  Came where as our Lord did rest.
And there they laid before the maid,
  Unto her Son, her God, and King,
Their offerings sweet, as was most meet,
  Unto so great a power to bring.

## VIII.

Now to him that hath redeem'd us,
    By his precious death and passion;
And us sinners so esteem'd us,
    To buy dearly this salvation.
Yield lasting fame, that still the name
    Of Jesus may be honour'd here;
And let us say that Christmas Day,
    Is still the best day in the year.

## CAROL VIII.

### I.

Let all that are to mirth inclin'd,
Consider well, and bear in mind,
What our good God for us has done,
In sending his beloved Son.

#### CHORUS.

For to redeem our souls from thrall,
Christ is the Saviour of us all.

### II.

Let all your songs and praises be,
Unto his Heavenly Majesty;
And evermore, amongst our mirth,
Remember Christ our Saviour's birth.

For to, &c.

### III.

The twenty-fifth day of December,
We have good cause for to remember;
In Bethlehem upon that morn,
There was the bless'd Messiah born.

For to, &c.

# CAROL 8

Let all &c:  Consider &c:

What &c:  In

Chorus

For &c:

Christ &c:

### IV.

The night before that happy tide,
The spotless virgin and her guide,
Were long time seeking up and down,
To find some lodging in the town.

> For to, &c.

### V.

But mark how all things came to pass,
The inn and lodgings filled was,
That they could find no room at all,
But in a silly ox's stall.——For to, &c.

### VI.

That night the Virgin Mary mild,
Was safe deliver'd of a child;
According unto Heav'n's decree,
Man's sweet salvation for to be.

> For to, &c.

### VII.

Near Bethlehem some Shepherds keep
Their flocks and herds of feeding sheep;
To whom God's Angel did appear,
Which put the Shepherds in great fear.

> For to, &c.

### VIII.

Prepare and go, the Angel said,
To Bethlehem, be not afraid;
There shall you find this blessed morn,
The princely babe, sweet Jesus born.

> For to, &c.

c

### IX.

With thankful heart and joyful mind,
The Shepherds went this babe to find,
And as the Heav'nly Angels told,
They did our Saviour Christ behold.

For to, &c.

### X.

Within a manger was he laid,
The Virgin Mary by him staid;
Attending on the Lord of life,
Being both mother, maid, and wife.

For to, &c.

### XI.

Three Eastern wise men from afar,
Directed by a glorious star;
Came boldly on, and made no stay,
Until they came where Jesus lay.

For to, &c.

### XII.

And being come unto the place,
Whereas the blessed Messiah was;
They humbly laid before his feet,
Their gifts of gold and odours sweet.

For to, &c.

### XIII.

See how the Lord of Heaven and earth,
Shew'd himself lowly in his birth;
A sweet example for mankind,
To learn to bear an humble mind.

For to, &c.

## XIV.

No costly robes nor rich attire,
Did Jesus Christ our Lord desire;
No music nor sweet harmony,
Till glorious music from on high

For to, &c.

## XV.

Did in melodious manner sing,
Praises unto our heav'nly King;
All honour, glory, might, and pow'r,
Be unto Christ our Saviour.——For to, &c.

## XVI.

If quires of Angels did rejoice,
Well may mankind with heart and voice
Sing praises to the God of Heav'n,
That unto us his Son has given.

For to redeem our souls from thrall,
Christ is the Saviour of us all.

**FINIS.**

London : Printed by J. Nichols and Son,
25, Parliament Street.